FARRAR
STRAUS
GIROUX

The Spirit Level

THE
SPIRIT
LEVEL

SEAMUS
HEANEY

Farrar Straus Giroux : New York

Library of Congress Cataloging-in-Publication Data
Heaney, Seamus.
The spirit level / Seamus Heaney.
p.   cm.
I. Title.
PR6058.E2S67   1996   821'.914—dc20   95-42585   CIP

For Helen Vendler

Notes and Acknowledgements

Acknowledgements are due to the editors of the following magazines where these poems first appeared: *Agenda, Agni Review, Antaeus, College Green, Gown, The Guardian, Harvard Review, Honest Ulsterman, Independent on Sunday, The Irish Times, London Review of Books, Mica, The New Republic, New Welsh Review, Notre Dame Review, Oxford Poetry, Parnassus, Poetry, Poetry & Audience, Poetry Ireland Review, P.N. Review, Soho Square, The Southern Review, Thinker Review, The Threepenny Review, TickleAce, The Times Literary Supplement, Verse, Verso.* 'At the Wellhead', 'Keeping Going', 'The Sharping Stone', 'Tollund' and section 5 of 'The Flight Path' were published in *The New Yorker*. 'The Flight Path' originally appeared in *P.N. Review 88*, a special issue celebrating Donald Davie's seventieth birthday. It is published here in memory of Donald Davie, who died in 1995. 'After Liberation' first appeared in *Turning Tides* (Story Line Press, 1994); 'The First Words' is a version of a poem by Marin Sorescu from a translation by Ioana Russell-Gebbett (previously printed in *The Biggest Egg in the World*, Bloodaxe, 1987).

Contents

The Spirit Level

The Rain Stick

for Beth and Rand

Upend the rain stick and what happens next
Is a music that you never would have known
To listen for. In a cactus stalk

Downpour, sluice-rush, spillage and backwash
Come flowing through. You stand there like a pipe
Being played by water, you shake it again lightly

And diminuendo runs through all its scales
Like a gutter stopping trickling. And now here comes
A sprinkle of drops out of the freshened leaves,

Then subtle little wets off grass and daisies;
Then glitter-drizzle, almost-breaths of air.
Upend the stick again. What happens next

Is undiminished for having happened once,
Twice, ten, a thousand times before.
Who cares if all the music that transpires

Is the fall of grit or dry seeds through a cactus?
You are like a rich man entering heaven
Through the ear of a raindrop. Listen now again.

To a Dutch Potter in Ireland

for Sonja Landweer

Then I entered a strongroom of vocabulary
Where words like urns that had come through the fire
Stood in their bone-dry alcoves next a kiln

And came away changed, like the guard who'd seen
The stone move in a diamond-blaze of air
Or the gates of horn behind the gates of clay.

1

The soils I knew ran dirty. River sand
Was the one clean thing that stayed itself
In that slabbery, clabbery, wintry, puddled ground.

Until I found Bann clay. Like wet daylight
Or viscous satin under the felt and frieze
Of humus layers. The true diatomite

Discovered in a little sucky hole,
Grey-blue, dull-shining, scentless, touchable—
Like the earth's old ointment box, sticky and cool.

At that stage you were swimming in the sea
Or running from it, luminous with plankton,
A nymph of phosphor by the Norder Zee,

A vestal of the goddess Silica,
She who is under grass and glass and ash
In the fiery heartlands of Ceramica.

We might have known each other then, in that
Cold gleam-life under ground and off the water.
Weird twins of puddle, paddle, pit-a-pat,

And might have done the small forbidden things—
Worked at mud-pies or gone too high on swings,
Played 'secrets' in the hedge or 'touching tongues'—

But did not, in the terrible event.
Night after night instead, in the Netherlands,
You watched the bombers kill; then, heaven-sent,

Came backlit from the fire through war and wartime
And ever after, every blessed time,
Through glazes of fired quartz and iron and lime.

And if glazes, as you say, bring down the sun,
Your potter's wheel is bringing up the earth.
Hosannah ex infernis. Burning wells.

Hosannah in clean sand and kaolin
And, 'now that the rye crop waves beside the ruins',
In ash-pits, oxides, shards and chlorophylls.

2. AFTER LIBERATION

[from the Dutch of J. C. Bloem (1887–1966)]

i

Sheer, bright-shining spring, spring as it used to be,
Cold in the morning, but as broad daylight
Swings open, the everlasting sky
Is a marvel to survivors.

In a pearly clarity that bathes the fields
Things as they were come back; slow horses
Plough the fallow, war rumbles away
In the near distance.

To have lived it through and now be free to give
Utterance, body and soul—to wake and know
Every time that it's gone and gone for good, the thing
That nearly broke you—

Is worth it all, the five years on the rack,
The fighting back, the being resigned, and not
One of the unborn will appreciate
Freedom like this ever.

ii

Turning tides, their regularities!
What is the heart, that it ever was afraid,

6

Knowing as it must know spring's release,
Shining heart, heart constant as a tide?

Omnipresent, imperturbable
Is the life that death springs from.
And complaint is wrong, the slightest complaint at all,
Now that the rye crop waves beside the ruins.

A Brigid's Girdle

for Adele

Last time I wrote I wrote from a rustic table
Under magnolias in South Carolina
As blossoms fell on me, and a white gable
As clean-lined as the prow of a white liner

Bisected sunlight in the sunlit yard.
I was glad of the early heat and the first quiet
I'd had for weeks. I heard the mocking bird
And a delicious, articulate

Flight of small plinkings from a dulcimer
Like feminine rhymes migrating to the north
Where you faced the music and the ache of summer
And earth's foreknowledge gathered in the earth.

Now it's St Brigid's Day and the first snowdrop
In County Wicklow, and this a Brigid's Girdle
I'm plaiting for you, an airy fairy hoop
(Like one of those old crinolines they'd trindle),

Twisted straw that's lifted in a circle
To handsel and to heal, a rite of spring
As strange and lightsome and traditional
As the motions you go through going through the thing.

Mint

It looked like a clump of small dusty nettles
Growing wild at the gable of the house
Beyond where we dumped our refuse and old bottles:
Unverdant ever, almost beneath notice.

But, to be fair, it also spelled promise
And newness in the back yard of our life
As if something callow yet tenacious
Sauntered in green alleys and grew rife.

The snip of scissor blades, the light of Sunday
Mornings when the mint was cut and loved:
My last things will be first things slipping from me.
Yet let all things go free that have survived.

Let the smells of mint go heady and defenceless
Like inmates liberated in that yard.
Like the disregarded ones we turned against
Because we'd failed them by our disregard.

A Sofa in the Forties

All of us on the sofa in a line, kneeling
Behind each other, eldest down to youngest,
Elbows going like pistons, for this was a train

And between the jamb-wall and the bedroom door
Our speed and distance were inestimable.
First we shunted, then we whistled, then

Somebody collected the invisible
For tickets and very gravely punched it
As carriage after carriage under us

Moved faster, *chooka-chook*, the sofa legs
Went giddy and the unreachable ones
Far out on the kitchen floor began to wave.

·

Ghost-train? Death-gondola? The carved, curved ends,
Black leatherette and ornate gauntness of it
Made it seem the sofa had achieved

Flotation. Its castors on tiptoe,
Its braid and fluent backboard gave it airs
Of superannuated pageantry:

When visitors endured it, straight-backed,
When it stood off in its own remoteness,
When the insufficient toys appeared on it

On Christmas mornings, it held out as itself,
Potentially heavenbound, earthbound for sure,
Among things that might add up or let you down.

                              •

We entered history and ignorance
Under the wireless shelf. *Yippee-i-ay*,
Sang 'The Riders of the Range'. HERE IS THE NEWS,

Said the absolute speaker. Between him and us
A great gulf was fixed where pronunciation
Reigned tyrannically. The aerial wire

Swept from a treetop down in through a hole
Bored in the windowframe. When it moved in wind,
The sway of language and its furtherings

Swept and swayed in us like nets in water
Or the abstract, lonely curve of distant trains
As we entered history and ignorance.

                              •

We occupied our seats with all our might,
Fit for the uncomfortableness.
Constancy was its own reward already.

Out in front, on the big upholstered arm,
Somebody craned to the side, driver or
Fireman, wiping his dry brow with the air

Of one who had run the gauntlet. We were
The last thing on his mind, it seemed; we sensed
A tunnel coming up where we'd pour through

Like unlit carriages through fields at night,
Our only job to sit, eyes straight ahead,
And be transported and make engine noise.

Keeping Going

for Hugh

The piper coming from far away is you
With a whitewash brush for a sporran
Wobbling round you, a kitchen chair
Upside down on your shoulder, your right arm
Pretending to tuck the bag beneath your elbow,
Your pop-eyes and big cheeks nearly bursting
With laughter, but keeping the drone going on
Interminably, between catches of breath.

·

The whitewash brush. An old blanched skirted thing
On the back of the byre door, biding its time
Until spring airs spelled lime in a work-bucket
And a potstick to mix it in with water.
Those smells brought tears to the eyes, we inhaled
A kind of greeny burning and thought of brimstone.
But the slop of the actual job
Of brushing walls, the watery grey
Being lashed on in broad swatches, then drying out
Whiter and whiter, all that worked like magic.
Where had we come from, what was this kingdom
We knew we'd been restored to? Our shadows
Moved on the wall and a tar border glittered
The full length of the house, a black divide
Like a freshly opened, pungent, reeking trench.

•

Piss at the gable, the dead will congregate.
But separately. The women after dark,
Hunkering there a moment before bedtime,
The only time the soul was let alone,
The only time that face and body calmed
In the eye of heaven.
                              Buttermilk and urine,
The pantry, the housed beasts, the listening bedroom.
We were all together there in a foretime,
In a knowledge that might not translate beyond
Those wind-heaved midnights we still cannot be sure
Happened or not. It smelled of hill-fort clay
And cattle dung. When the thorn tree was cut down
You broke your arm. I shared the dread
When a strange bird perched for days on the byre roof.

•

That scene, with Macbeth helpless and desperate
In his nightmare—when he meets the hags again
And sees the apparitions in the pot—
I felt at home with that one all right. Hearth,
Steam and ululation, the smoky hair
Curtaining a cheek. 'Don't go near bad boys
In that college that you're bound for. Do you hear me?

Do you hear me speaking to you? Don't forget!'
And then the potstick quickening the gruel,
The steam crown swirled, everything intimate
And fear-swathed brightening for a moment,
Then going dull and fatal and away.

·

Grey matter like gruel flecked with blood
In spatters on the whitewash. A clean spot
Where his head had been, other stains subsumed
In the parched wall he leant his back against
That morning like any other morning,
Part-time reservist, toting his lunch-box.
A car came slow down Castle Street, made the halt,
Crossed the Diamond, slowed again and stopped
Level with him, although it was not his lift.
And then he saw an ordinary face
For what it was and a gun in his own face.
His right leg was hooked back, his sole and heel
Against the wall, his right knee propped up steady,
So he never moved, just pushed with all his might
Against himself, then fell past the tarred strip,
Feeding the gutter with his copious blood.

·

My dear brother, you have good stamina.
You stay on where it happens. Your big tractor
Pulls up at the Diamond, you wave at people,
You shout and laugh about the revs, you keep
Old roads open by driving on the new ones.
You called the piper's sporrans whitewash brushes
And then dressed up and marched us through the
    kitchen,
But you cannot make the dead walk or right wrong.
I see you at the end of your tether sometimes,
In the milking parlour, holding yourself up
Between two cows until your turn goes past,
Then coming to in the smell of dung again
And wondering, is this all? As it was
In the beginning, is now and shall be?
Then rubbing your eyes and seeing our old brush
Up on the byre door, and keeping going.

Two Lorries

It's raining on black coal and warm wet ashes.
There are tyre-marks in the yard, Agnew's old lorry
Has all its cribs down and Agnew the coalman
With his Belfast accent's sweet-talking my mother.
Would she ever go to a film in Magherafelt?
But it's raining and he still has half the load

To deliver farther on. This time the lode
Our coal came from was silk-black, so the ashes
Will be the silkiest white. The Magherafelt
(Via Toomebridge) bus goes by. The half-stripped lorry
With its emptied, folded coal-bags moves my mother:
The tasty ways of a leather-aproned coalman!

And films no less! The conceit of a coalman . . .
She goes back in and gets out the black lead
And emery paper, this nineteen-forties mother,
All business round her stove, half-wiping ashes
With a backhand from her cheek as the bolted lorry
Gets revved and turned and heads for Magherafelt

And the last delivery. Oh, Magherafelt!
Oh, dream of red plush and a city coalman
As time fastforwards and a different lorry
Groans into shot, up Broad Street, with a payload
That will blow the bus station to dust and ashes . . .
After that happened, I'd a vision of my mother,

A revenant on the bench where I would meet her
In that cold-floored waiting-room in Magherafelt,
Her shopping bags full up with shovelled ashes.
Death walked out past her like a dust-faced coalman
Refolding body-bags, plying his load
Empty upon empty, in a flurry

Of motes and engine-revs, but which lorry
Was it now? Young Agnew's or that other,
Heavier, deadlier one, set to explode
In a time beyond her time in Magherafelt . . .
So tally bags and sweet-talk darkness, coalman.
Listen to the rain spit in new ashes

As you heft a load of dust that was Magherafelt,
Then reappear from your lorry as my mother's
Dreamboat coalman filmed in silk-white ashes.

Damson

Gules and cement dust. A matte tacky blood
On the bricklayer's knuckles, like the damson stain
That seeped through his packed lunch.
                                        A full hod stood
Against the mortared wall, his big bright trowel
In his left hand (for once) was pointing down
As he marvelled at his right, held high and raw:
King of the castle, scaffold-stepper, shown
Bleeding to the world.
                        Wound that I saw
In glutinous colour fifty years ago—
Damson as omen, weird, a dream to read—
Is weeping with the held-at-arm's-length dead
From everywhere and nowhere, here and now.

                    .

Over and over, the slur, the scrape and mix
As he trowelled and retrowelled and laid down
Courses of glum mortar. Then the bricks
Jiggled and settled, tocked and tapped in line.
I loved especially the trowel's shine,
Its edge and apex always coming clean
And brightening itself by mucking in.
It looked light but felt heavy as a weapon,
Yet when he lifted it there was no strain.
It was all point and skim and float and glisten

Until he washed and lapped it tight in sacking
Like a cult blade that had to be kept hidden.

·

Ghosts with their tongues out for a lick of blood
Are crowding up the ladder, all unhealed,
And some of them still rigged in bloody gear.
Drive them back to the doorstep or the road
Where they lay in their own blood once, in the hot
Nausea and last gasp of dear life.
Trowel-wielder, woundie, drive them off
Like Odysseus in Hades lashing out
With his sword that dug the trench and cut the throat
Of the sacrificial lamb.
                                    But not like him—
Builder, not sacker, your shield the mortar board—
Drive them back to the wine-dark taste of home,
The smell of damsons simmering in a pot,
Jam ladled thick and steaming down the sunlight.

Weighing In

The 56 lb. weight. A solid iron
Unit of negation. Stamped and cast
With an inset, rung-thick, moulded, short crossbar

For a handle. Squared-off and harmless-looking
Until you tried to lift it, then a socket-ripping,
Life-belittling force—

Gravity's black box, the immovable
Stamp and squat and square-root of dead weight.
Yet balance it

Against another one placed on a weighbridge—
On a well-adjusted, freshly greased weighbridge—
And everything trembled, flowed with give and take.

.

And this is all the good tidings amount to:
This principle of bearing, bearing up
And bearing out, just having to

Balance the intolerable in others
Against our own, having to abide
Whatever we settled for and settled into

Against our better judgement. Passive
Suffering makes the world go round.
Peace on earth, men of good will, all that

Holds good only as long as the balance holds,
The scales ride steady and the angels' strain
Prolongs itself at an unearthly pitch.

·

To refuse the other cheek. To cast the stone.
Not to do so some time, not to break with
The obedient one you hurt yourself into

Is to fail the hurt, the self, the ingrown rule.
Prophesy who struck thee! When soldiers mocked
Blindfolded Jesus and he didn't strike back

They were neither shamed nor edified, although
Something was made manifest—the power
Of power not exercised, of hope inferred

By the powerless forever. Still, for Jesus' sake,
Do me a favour, would you, just this once?
Prophesy, give scandal, cast the stone.

·

Two sides to every question, yes, yes, yes . . .
But every now and then, just weighing in
Is what it must come down to, and without

Any self-exculpation or self-pity.
Alas, one night when follow-through was called for
And a quick hit would have fairly rankled,

You countered that it was my narrowness
That kept me keen, so got a first submission.
I held back when I should have drawn blood

And that way *(mea culpa)* lost an edge.
A deep mistaken chivalry, old friend.
At this stage only foul play cleans the slate.

St Kevin and the Blackbird

And then there was St Kevin and the blackbird.
The saint is kneeling, arms stretched out, inside
His cell, but the cell is narrow, so

One turned-up palm is out the window, stiff
As a crossbeam, when a blackbird lands
And lays in it and settles down to nest.

Kevin feels the warm eggs, the small breast, the tucked
Neat head and claws and, finding himself linked
Into the network of eternal life,

Is moved to pity: now he must hold his hand
Like a branch out in the sun and rain for weeks
Until the young are hatched and fledged and flown.

•

And since the whole thing's imagined anyhow,
Imagine being Kevin. Which is he?
Self-forgetful or in agony all the time

From the neck on out down through his hurting
        forearms?
Are his fingers sleeping? Does he still feel his knees?
Or has the shut-eyed blank of underearth

Crept up through him? Is there distance in his head?
Alone and mirrored clear in love's deep river,
'To labour and not to seek reward,' he prays,

A prayer his body makes entirely
For he has forgotten self, forgotten bird
And on the riverbank forgotten the river's name.

The Flight Path

The first fold first, then more foldovers drawn
Tighter and neater every time until
The whole of the paper got itself reduced
To a pleated square he'd take up by two corners,
Then hold like a promise he had the power to break
But never did.
            A dove rose in my breast
Every time my father's hands came clean
With a paper boat between them, ark in air,
The lines of it as taut as a pegged tent:
High-sterned, splay-bottomed, the little pyramid
At the centre every bit as hollow
As a part of me that sank because it knew
The whole thing would go soggy once you launched it.

Equal and opposite, the part that lifts
Into those *full-starred heavens that winter sees*
When I stand in Wicklow under the flight path
Of a late jet out of Dublin, its risen light
Winking ahead of what it hauls away:
Heavy engine noise and its abatement
Widening far back down, a wake through starlight.

The sycamore speaks in sycamore from darkness,
The light behind my shoulder's cottage lamplight.
I'm in the doorway early in the night,
Standing-in in myself for all of those
The stance perpetuates: the stay-at-homes
Who leant against the jamb and watched and waited,
The ones we learned to love by waving back at
Or coming towards again in different clothes
They were slightly shy of.
                                    Who never once forgot
A name or a face, nor looked down suddenly
As the plane was reaching cruising altitude
To realize that the house they'd just passed over—
Too far back now to see—was the same house
They'd left an hour before, still kissing, kissing,
As the taxi driver loaded up the cases.

3

Up and away. The buzz from duty free.
Black Velvet. Bourbon. Love letters on high.
The spacewalk of Manhattan. The re-entry.

Then California. Laid-back Tiburon.
Burgers at Sam's, deck-tables and champagne,
Plus a wall-eyed, hard-baked seagull looking on.

Again re-entry. Vows revowed. And off—
Reculer pour sauter, within one year of
Coming back, less long goodbye than stand-off.

So to Glanmore. Glanmore. Glanmore. Glanmore.
At bay, at one, at work, at risk and sure.
Covert and pad. Oak, bay and sycamore.

Jet-sitting next. Across and across and across.
Westering, eastering, the jumbo a school bus,
'The Yard' a cross between the farm and campus,

A holding pattern and a tautening purchase—
Sweeney astray in home truths out of Horace:
Skies change, not cares, for those who cross the seas.

4

The following for the record, in the light
Of everything before and since:
One bright May morning, nineteen-seventy-nine,
Just off the red-eye special from New York,
I'm on the train for Belfast. Plain, simple
Exhilaration at being back: the sea
At Skerries, the nuptial hawthorn bloom,
The trip north taking sweet hold like a chain

On every bodily sprocket.
                    Enter then—
As if he were some *film noir* border guard—
Enter this one I'd last met in a dream,
More grimfaced now than in the dream itself
When he'd flagged me down at the side of a mountain
      road,
Come up and leant his elbow on the roof
And explained through the open window of the car
That all I'd have to do was drive a van
Carefully in to the next customs post
At Pettigo, switch off, get out as if
I were on my way with dockets to the office—
But then instead I'd walk ten yards more down
Towards the main street and get in with—here
Another schoolfriend's name, a wink and smile,
I'd know him all right, he'd be in a Ford
And I'd be home in three hours' time, as safe
As houses . . .
            So he enters and sits down
Opposite and goes for me head on.
'When, for fuck's sake, are you going to write
Something for us?' 'If I do write something,
Whatever it is, I'll be writing for myself.'
And that was that. Or words to that effect.

The gaol walls all those months were smeared with
    shite.
Out of Long Kesh after his dirty protest
The red eyes were the eyes of Ciaran Nugent
Like something out of Dante's scurfy hell,
Drilling their way through the rhymes and images
Where I too walked behind the righteous Virgil,
As safe as houses and translating freely:
When he had said all this, his eyes rolled
And his teeth, like a dog's teeth clamping round a bone,
Bit into the skull and again took hold.

5

When I answered that I came from 'far away',
The policeman at the roadblock snapped, 'Where's
    that?'
He'd only half-heard what I said and thought
It was the name of some place up the country.

And now it is—both where I have been living
And where I left—a distance still to go
Like starlight that is light years on the go
From far away and takes light years arriving.

6

Out of the blue then, the sheer exaltation
Of remembering climbing zig-zag up warm steps
To the hermit's eyrie above Rocamadour.
Crows sailing high and close, a lizard pulsing
On gravel at my feet, its front legs set
Like the jointed front struts of a moon vehicle.
And bigly, softly as the breath of life
In a breath of air, a lime-green butterfly
Crossing the pilgrims' sunstruck *via crucis*.

Eleven in the morning. I made a note:
'Rock-lover, loner, sky-sentry, all hail!'
And somewhere the dove rose. And kept on rising.

An Invocation

[*Hugh MacDiarmid (1892–1978)*]

Incline to me, MacDiarmid, out of Shetland,
Stone-eyed from stone-gazing, sobered up
And thrawn. Not the old vigilante

Of the chimney corner, having us on,
Setting us off, the drinkers' drinker; no,
Incline as the sage of winds that flout the rock face,

As gull stalled in the sea breeze, gatekeeper
Of the open gates behind the brows of birds—
Not to hear me take back smart remarks

About your MacGonagallish propensities—
For I do not—but I add in middle age:
I underprized your far-out, blathering genius.

·

Those years in the shore-view house, especially.
More intellectual billygoat than scapegoat,
Beyond the stony limits, writing-mad.

That pride of being tested. Of solitude.
Your big pale forehead in the window glass
Like the earth's curve on the sea's curve to the north.

At your wits' end then, always on the go
To the beach and back, taking heady bearings
Between the horizon and the dictionary,

Hard-liner on the rock face of the old
Questions and answers, to which I add my own:
'Who is my neighbour? My neighbour is all mankind.'

.

And if you won't incline, endure
At an embraced distance. Be the wee
Contrary stormcock that you always were,

The weather-eye of a poetry like the weather,
A shifting force, a factor factored in
Whether it prevails or not, constantly

A function of its time and place
And sometimes of our own. Never, at any rate,
Beyond us, even when outlandish.

In the accent, in the idiom, in
The idea like a thistle in the wind,
A catechism worth repeating always.

Mycenae Lookout

for Cynthia and Dimitri Hadzi

The ox is on my tongue.
—AESCHYLUS, *Agamemnon*

1. THE WATCHMAN'S WAR

Some people wept, and not for sorrow—joy
That the king had armed and upped and sailed for Troy,
But inside me like struck sound in a gong
That killing-fest, the life-warp and world-wrong
It brought to pass, still augured and endured.
I'd dream of blood in bright webs in a ford,
Of bodies raining down like tattered meat
On top of me asleep—and me the lookout
The queen's command had posted and forgotten,
The blind spot her farsightedness relied on.
And then the ox would lurch against the gong
And deaden it and I would feel my tongue
Like the dropped gangplank of a cattle truck,
Trampled and rattled, running piss and muck,
All swimmy-trembly as the lick of fire,
A victory beacon in an abattoir . . .
Next thing then I would waken at a loss,
For all the world a sheepdog stretched in grass,
Exposed to what I knew, still honour-bound
To concentrate attention out beyond
The city and the border, on that line

Where the blaze would leap the hills when Troy had
    fallen.

My sentry work was fate, a home to go to,
An in-between-times that I had to row through
Year after year: when the mist would start
To lift off fields and inlets, when morning light
Would open like the grain of light being split,
Day in, day out, I'd come alive again,
Silent and sunned as an esker on a plain,
Up on my elbows, gazing, biding time
In my outpost on the roof . . . What was to come
Out of that ten years' wait that was the war
Flawed the black mirror of my frozen stare.
If a god of justice had reached down from heaven
For a strong beam to hang his scale-pans on
He would have found me tensed and ready-made.
I balanced between destiny and dread
And saw it coming, clouds bloodshot with the red
Of victory fires, the raw wound of that dawn
Igniting and erupting, bearing down
Like lava on a fleeing population . . .
Up on my elbows, head back, shutting out
The agony of Clytemnestra's love-shout
That rose through the palace like the yell of troops
Hurled by King Agamemnon from the ships.

2. CASSANDRA

No such thing
as innocent
bystanding.

Her soiled vest,
her little breasts,
her clipped, devast-

ated, scabbed
punk head,
the char-eyed

famine gawk—
she looked
camp-fucked

and simple.
People
could feel

a missed
trueness in them
focus,

a homecoming
in her dropped-wing,
half-calculating

bewilderment.
No such thing
as innocent.

Old King Cock-
of-the-Walk
was back,

King Kill-
the-Child-
and-Take-

What-Comes,
King Agamem-
non's drum-

balled, old buck's
stride was back.
And then her Greek

words came,
a lamb
at lambing time,

bleat of clair-
voyant dread,
the gene-hammer

and tread
of the roused god.
And a result-

ant shock desire
in bystanders
to do it to her

there and then.
Little rent
cunt of their guilt:

in she went
to the knife,
to the killer wife,

to the net over
her and her slaver,
the Troy reaver,

saying, 'A wipe
of the sponge,
that's it.

The shadow-hinge
swings unpredict-
ably and the light's

blanked out.'

3 · HIS DAWN VISION

Cities of grass. Fort walls. The dumbstruck palace.
I'd come to with the night wind on my face,
Agog, alert again, but far, far less

Focused on victory than I should have been—
Still isolated in my old disdain
Of claques who always needed to be seen

And heard as the true Argives. Mouth athletes,
Quoting the oracle and quoting dates,
Petitioning, accusing, taking votes.

No element that should have carried weight
Out of the grievous distance would translate.
Our war stalled in the pre-articulate.

The little violets' heads bowed on their stems,
The pre-dawn gossamers, all dew and scrim
And star-lace, it was more through them

I felt the beating of the huge time-wound
We lived inside. My soul wept in my hand
When I would touch them, my whole being rained

Down on myself, I saw cities of grass,
Valleys of longing, tombs, a wind-swept brightness,
And far-off, in a hilly, ominous place,

Small crowds of people watching as a man
Jumped a fresh earth-wall and another ran
Amorously, it seemed, to strike him down.

4. THE NIGHTS

They both needed to talk,
pretending what they needed
was my advice. Behind backs
each one of them confided
it was sexual overload
every time they did it—
and indeed from the beginning
(a child could have hardly missed it)
their real life was the bed.

The king should have been told,
but who was there to tell him
if not myself? I willed them
to cease and break the hold
of my cross-purposed silence
but still kept on, all smiles
to Aegisthus every morning,
much favoured and self-loathing.
The roof was like an eardrum.

The ox's tons of dumb
inertia stood, head-down
and motionless as a herm.
Atlas, watchmen's patron,
would come into my mind,
the only other one

up at all hours, ox-bowed
under his yoke of cloud
out there at the world's end.

The loft-floor where the gods
and goddesses took lovers
and made out endlessly
successfully, those thuds
and moans through the cloud cover
were wholly on his shoulders.
Sometimes I thought of us
apotheosized to boulders
called Aphrodite's Pillars.

High and low in those days
hit their stride together.
When the captains in the horse
felt Helen's hand caress
its wooden boards and belly
they nearly rode each other.
But in the end Troy's mothers
bore their brunt in alley,
bloodied cot and bed.
The war put all men mad,
horned, horsed or roof-posted,
the boasting and the bested.

My own mind was a bull-pen
where horned King Agamemnon
had stamped his weight in gold.
But when hills broke into flame
and the queen wailed on and came,
it was the king I sold.
I moved beyond bad faith:
for his bullion bars, his bonus
was a rope-net and a blood-bath.
And the peace had come upon us.

At Troy, at Athens, what I most clearly
see and nearly smell
is the fresh water.

A filled bath, still unentered
and unstained, waiting behind housewalls
that the far cries of the butchered on the plain

keep dying into, until the hero comes
surging in incomprehensibly
to be attended to and be alone,

stripped to the skin, blood-plastered, moaning
and rocking, splashing, dozing off,
accommodated as if he were a stranger.

And the well at Athens too.
Or rather that old lifeline leading up
and down from the Acropolis

to the well itself, a set of timber steps
slatted in between the sheer cliff face
and a free-standing, covering spur of rock,

secret staircase the defenders knew
and the invaders found, where what was to be
Greek met Greek,

the ladder of the future
and the past, besieger and besieged,
the treadmill of assault

turned waterwheel, the rungs of stealth
and habit all the one
bare foot extended, searching.

And then this ladder of our own that ran
deep into a well-shaft being sunk
in broad daylight, men puddling at the source

through tawny mud, then coming back up
deeper in themselves for having been there
like discharged soldiers testing the safe ground,

finders, keepers, seers of fresh water
in the bountiful round mouths of iron pumps
and gushing taps.

The First Words

[*from the Romanian of Marin Sorescu*]

The first words got polluted
Like river water in the morning
Flowing with the dirt
Of blurbs and the front pages.
My only drink is meaning from the deep brain,
What the birds and the grass and the stones drink.
Let everything flow
Up to the four elements,
Up to water and earth and fire and air.

The Gravel Walks

River gravel. In the beginning, that.
High summer, and the angler's motorbike
Deep in roadside flowers, like a fallen knight
Whose ghost we'd lately questioned: 'Any luck?'

As the engines of the world prepared, green nuts
Dangled and clustered closer to the whirlpool.
The trees dipped down. The flints and sandstone-bits
Worked themselves smooth and smaller in a sparkle

Of shallow, hurrying barley-sugar water
Where minnows schooled that we scared when we
     played—
An eternity that ended once a tractor
Dropped its link-box in the gravel bed

And cement mixers began to come to life
And men in dungarees, like captive shades,
Mixed concrete, loaded, wheeled, turned, wheeled, as if
The Pharaoh's brickyards burned inside their heads.

·

Hoard and praise the verity of gravel.
Gems for the undeluded. Milt of earth.
Its plain, champing song against the shovel
Soundtests and sandblasts words like 'honest worth'.

Beautiful in or out of the river,
The kingdom of gravel was inside you too—
Deep down, far back, clear water running over
Pebbles of caramel, hailstone, mackerel-blue.

But the actual washed stuff kept you slow and steady
As you went stooping with your barrow full
Into an absolution of the body,
The shriven life tired bones and marrow feel.

So walk on air against your better judgement
Establishing yourself somewhere in between
Those solid batches mixed with grey cement
And a tune called 'The Gravel Walks' that conjures
    green.

Whitby-sur-Moyola

Caedmon too I was lucky to have known,
Back *in situ* there with his full bucket
And armfuls of clean straw, the perfect yardman,
Unabsorbed in what he had to do
But doing it perfectly, and watching you.
He had worked his angel stint. He was hard as nails
And all that time he'd been poeting with the harp
His real gift was the big ignorant roar
He could still let out of him, just bogging in
As if the sacred subjects were a herd
That had broken out and needed rounding up.
I never saw him once with his hands joined
Unless it was a case of eyes to heaven
And the quick sniff and test of fingertips
After he'd passed them through a sick beast's water.
Oh, Caedmon was the real thing all right.

The Thimble

In the House of Carnal Murals
The painter used it to hold a special red
He touched the lips and freshest bite-marks with.

2

Until the Reformation, it was revered
As a relic of St Adaman.
The workers in a certain foundry cast
A bell, so heavy, it was said,
No apparatus could lift it to the belltower—
And afterwards were stricken one by one
With a kind of sleeping sickness.
In the middle of the fiery delirium
Of metal pouring, they would all fall quiet
And see green waterweed and stepping stones
Across the molten bronze.
So Adaman arrived and blessed their hands
And eyes and cured them, but at that hour
The bell too shrank miraculously
And henceforth was known to the faithful
And registered in the canons' inventory
As Adaman's Thimble.

3

Was this the measure of the sweetest promise,
The dipped thirst-brush, the dew of paradise
That would flee my tongue when they said 'A
    thimbleful'?

4

    Now a teenager
    With shaved head
    And translucent shoulders
    Wears it for a nipple-cap.

5

And so on.

The Butter-Print

Who carved on the butter-print's round open face
A cross-hatched head of rye, all jags and bristles?
Why should soft butter bear that sharp device
As if its breast were scored with slivered glass?

When I was small I swallowed an awn of rye.
My throat was like standing crop probed by a scythe.
I felt the edge slide and the point stick deep
Until, when I coughed and coughed and coughed it up,

My breathing came dawn-cold, so clear and sudden
I might have been inhaling airs from heaven
Where healed and martyred Agatha stares down
At the relic knife as I stared at the awn.

Remembered Columns

The solid letters of the world grew airy.
The marble serifs, the clearly blocked uprights
Built upon rocks and set upon the heights
Rose like remembered columns in a story

About the Virgin's house that rose and flew
And landed on the hilltop at Loreto.
I lift my eyes in a light-headed credo,
Discovering what survives translation true.

'Poet's Chair'

for Carolyn Mulholland

Leonardo said: the sun has never
Seen a shadow. Now watch the sculptor move
Full circle round her next work, like a lover
In the sphere of shifting angles and fixed love.

1

Angling shadows of itself are what
Your 'Poet's Chair' stands to and rises out of
In its sun-stalked inner-city courtyard.
On the *qui vive* all the time, its four legs land
On their feet—cat's-foot, goat-foot, big soft splay-foot too;
Its straight back sprouts two bronze and leafy saplings.
Every flibbertigibbet in the town,
Old birds and boozers, late-night pissers, kissers,
All have a go at sitting on it some time.
It's the way the air behind them's winged and full,
The way a graft has seized their shoulder-blades
That makes them happy. Once out of nature,
They're going to come back in leaf and bloom
And angel step. Or something like that. *Leaves*
On a bloody chair! Would you believe it?

Next thing I see the chair in a white prison
With Socrates sitting on it, bald as a coot,
Discoursing in bright sunlight with his friends.
His time is short. The day his trial began
A verdant boat sailed from Apollo's shrine
In Delos, for the annual rite
Of commemoration. Until its wreathed
And creepered rigging re-enters Athens
Harbour, the city's life is holy.
No executions. No hemlock bowl. No tears
And none now as the poison does its work
And the expert jailer talks the company through
The stages of the numbness. Socrates
At the centre of the city and the day
Has proved the soul immortal. The bronze leaves
Cannot believe their ears, it is so silent.
Soon Crito will have to close his eyes and mouth,
But for the moment everything's an ache
Deferred, foreknown, imagined and most real.

3

My father's ploughing one, two, three, four sides
Of the lea ground where I sit all-seeing

At centre field, my back to the thorn tree
They never cut. The horses are all hoof
And burnished flank, I am all foreknowledge.
Of the poem as a ploughshare that turns time
Up and over. Of the chair in leaf
The fairy thorn is entering for the future.
Of being here for good in every sense.

The Swing

Fingertips just tipping you would send you
Every bit as far—once you got going—
As a big push in the back.
                              Sooner or later,
We all learned one by one to go sky high,
Backward and forward in the open shed,
Toeing and rowing and jackknifing through air.

·

Not Fragonard. Nor Brueghel. It was more
Hans Memling's light of heaven off green grass,
Light over fields and hedges, the shed-mouth
Sunstruck and expectant, the bedding-straw
Piled to one side, like a Nativity
Foreground and background waiting for the figures.
And then, in the middle ground, the swing itself
With an old lopsided sack in the loop of it,
Perfectly still, hanging like pulley-slack,
A lure let down to tempt the soul to rise.

·

Even so, we favoured the earthbound. She
Sat there as majestic as an empress
Steeping her swollen feet one at a time
In the enamel basin, feeding it
Every now and again with an opulent

Steaming arc from a kettle on the floor
Beside her. The plout of that was music
To our ears, her smile a mitigation.
Whatever light the goddess had once shone
Around her favourite coming from the bath
Was what was needed then: there should have been
Fresh linen, ministrations by attendants,
Procession and amazement. Instead, she took
Each rolled elastic stocking and drew it on
Like the life she would not fail and was not
Meant for. And once, when she'd scoured the basin,
She came and sat to please us on the swing,
Neither out of place nor in her element,
Just tempted by it for a moment only,
Half-retrieving something half-confounded.
Instinctively we knew to let her be.

·

To start up by yourself, you hitched the rope
Against your backside and backed on into it
Until it tautened, then tiptoed and drove off
As hard as possible. You hurled a gathered thing
From the small of your own back into the air.
Your head swept low, you heard the whole shed creak.

·

We all learned one by one to go sky high.
Then townlands vanished into aerodromes,
Hiroshima made light of human bones,
Concorde's neb migrated towards the future.
So who were we to want to hang back there
In spite of all?
                    In spite of all, we sailed
Beyond ourselves and over and above
The rafters aching in our shoulder-blades,
The give and take of branches in our arms.

The Poplar

Wind shakes the big poplar, quicksilvering
The whole tree in a single sweep.
What bright scale fell and left this needle quivering?
What loaded balances have come to grief?

Two Stick Drawings

Claire O'Reilly used her granny's stick—
A crook-necked one—to snare the highest briars
That always grew the ripest blackberries.
When it came to gathering, Persephone
Was in the halfpenny place compared to Claire.
She'd trespass and climb gates and walk the railway
Where sootflakes blew into convolvulus
And the train tore past with the stoker yelling
Like a balked king from his iron chariot.

With its drover's canes and blackthorns and ashplants,
The ledge of the back seat of my father's car
Had turned into a kind of stick-shop window,
But the only one who ever window-shopped
Was Jim of the hanging jaw, for Jim was simple
And rain or shine he'd make his desperate rounds
From windscreen to back window, hands held up
To both sides of his face, peering and groaning.
So every now and then the sticks would be
Brought out for him and stood up one by one
Against the front mudguard; and one by one
Jim would take the measure of them, sight
And wield and slice and poke and parry
The unhindering air; until he found

The true extension of himself in one
That made him jubilant. He'd run and crow,
Stooped forward, with his right elbow stuck out
And the stick held horizontal to the ground,
Angled across in front of him, as if
He were leashed to it and it drew him on
Like a harness rod of the inexorable.

A Call

'Hold on,' she said, 'I'll just run out and get him.
The weather here's so good, he took the chance
To do a bit of weeding.'
                                    So I saw him
Down on his hands and knees beside the leek rig,
Touching, inspecting, separating one
Stalk from the other, gently pulling up
Everything not tapered, frail and leafless,
Pleased to feel each little weed-root break,
But rueful also . . .

                            Then found myself listening to
The amplified grave ticking of hall clocks
Where the phone lay unattended in a calm
Of mirror glass and sunstruck pendulums . . .

And found myself then thinking: if it were nowadays,
This is how Death would summon Everyman.

Next thing he spoke and I nearly said I loved him.

The Errand

'On you go now! Run, son, like the devil
And tell your mother to try
To find me a bubble for the spirit level
And a new knot for this tie.'

But still he was glad, I know, when I stood my ground,
Putting it up to him
With a smile that trumped his smile and his fool's
        errand,
Waiting for the next move in the game.

A Dog Was Crying Tonight
in Wicklow Also

in memory of Donatus Nwoga

When human beings found out about death
They sent the dog to Chukwu with a message:
They wanted to be let back to the house of life.
They didn't want to end up lost forever
Like burnt wood disappearing into smoke
Or ashes that get blown away to nothing.
Instead they saw their souls in a flock at twilight
Cawing and headed back for the same old roosts
And the same bright airs and wing-stretchings each
    morning.
Death would be like a night spent in the wood:
At first light they'd be back in the house of life.
(The dog was meant to tell all this to Chukwu.)

But death and human beings took second place
When he trotted off the path and started barking
At another dog in broad daylight just barking
Back at him from the far bank of a river.

And that is how the toad reached Chukwu first,
The toad who'd overheard in the beginning
What the dog was meant to tell. 'Human beings,' he
    said
(And here the toad was trusted absolutely),
'Human beings want death to last forever.'

66

Then Chukwu saw the people's souls in birds
Coming towards him like black spots off the sunset
To a place where there would be neither roosts nor
     trees
Nor any way back to the house of life.
And his mind reddened and darkened all at once
And nothing that the dog would tell him later
Could change that vision. Great chiefs and great loves
In obliterated light, the toad in mud,
The dog crying out all night behind the corpse house.

M.

When the deaf phonetician spread his hand
Over the dome of a speaker's skull
He could tell which diphthong and which vowel
By the bone vibrating to the sound.

A globe stops spinning. I set my palm
On a contour cold as permafrost
And imagine axle-hum and the steadfast
Russian of Osip Mandelstam.

An Architect

He fasted on the doorstep of his gift,
Exacting more, minding the boulder
And the raked zen gravel. But no slouch either

Whenever it came to whiskey, whether to
Lash into it or just to lash it out.
Courtly always, and rapt, and astonishing,

Like the day on the beach when he stepped out of his
        clothes
And waded along beside us in his pelt
Speculating, intelligent and lanky,

Taking things in his Elysian stride,
Talking his way back into sites and truths
The art required and his life came down to:

Blue slate and whitewash, shadow-lines, projections,
Things at once apparent and transparent,
Clean-edged, fine-drawn, drawn-out, redrawn,
        remembered . . .

Exit now, in his tweeds, down an aisle between
Drawing boards as far as the eye can see
To where it can't until he sketches where.

The Sharping Stone

In an apothecary's chest of drawers,
Sweet cedar that we'd purchased second hand,
In one of its weighty deep-sliding recesses
I found the sharping stone that was to be
Our gift to him. Still in its wrapping paper.
Like a baton of black light I'd failed to pass.

.

Airless cinder-depths. But all the same,
The way it lay there, it wakened something too . . .
I thought of us that evening on the logs,
Flat on our backs, the pair of us, parallel,
Supported head to heel, arms straight, eyes front,
Listening to the rain drip off the trees
And saying nothing, braced to the damp bark.
What possessed us? The bare, lopped loveliness
Of those two winter trunks, the way they seemed
Prepared for launching, at right angles across
A causeway of short fence-posts set like rollers.
Neither of us spoke. The puddles waited.
The workers had gone home, saws fallen silent.
And next thing down we lay, babes in the wood,
Gazing up at the flood-face of the sky
Until it seemed a flood was carrying us
Out of the forest park, feet first, eyes front,

Out of November, out of middle age,
Together, out, across the Sea of Moyle.

•

Sarcophage des époux. In terra cotta.
Etruscan couple shown side by side,
Recumbent on left elbows, husband pointing
With his right arm and watching where he points,
Wife in front, her earrings in, her braids
Down to her waist, taking her sexual ease.
He is all eyes, she is all brow and dream,
Her right forearm and hand held out as if
Some bird she sees in her deep inward gaze
Might be about to roost there. Domestic
Love, the artist thought, warm tones and property,
The frangibility of terra cotta . . .
Which is how they figured on the colour postcard
(Louvre, Département des Antiquités)
That we'd sent him once, then found among his
      things.

•

He loved inspired mistakes: his Spanish grandson's
English transliteration, thanking him
For a boat trip: 'That was a marvellous
Walk on the water, Granddad.' And indeed

He walked on air himself, never more so
Than when he had been widowed and the youth
In him, the athlete who had wooed her—
Breasting tapes and clearing the high bars—
Grew lightsome once again. Going at eighty
On the bendiest roads, going for broke
At every point-to-point and poker-school,
'He commenced his wild career' a second time
And not a bother on him. Smoked like a train
And took the power mower in his stride.
Flirted and vaunted. Set fire to his bed.
Fell from a ladder. Learned to microwave.

                    ·

So set the drawer on freshets of thaw water
And place the unused sharping stone inside it:
To be found next summer on a riverbank
Where scythes once hung all night in alder trees
And mowers played dawn scherzos on the blades,
Their arms like harpists' arms, one drawing towards,
One sweeping the bright rim of the extreme.

The Strand

The dotted line my father's ashplant made
On Sandymount Strand
Is something else the tide won't wash away.

The Walk

Glamoured the road, the day, and him and her
And everywhere they took me. When we stepped out
Cobbles were riverbed, the Sunday air
A high stream-roof that moved in silence over
Rhododendrons in full bloom, foxgloves
And hemlock, robin-run-the-hedge, the hedge
With its deckled ivy and thick shadows—
Until the riverbed itself appeared,
Gravelly, shallowy, summery with pools,
And made a world rim that was not for crossing.
Love brought me that far by the hand, without
The slightest doubt or irony, dry-eyed
And knowledgeable, contrary as be damned;
Then just kept standing there, not letting go.

.

So here is another longshot. Black and white.
A negative this time, in dazzle-dark,
Smudge and pallor where we make out you and me,
The selves we struggled with and struggled out of,
Two shades who have consumed each other's fire,
Two flames in sunlight that can sear and singe,
But seem like wisps of enervated air,
After-wavers, feathery ether-shifts . . .
Yet apt still to rekindle suddenly
If we find along the way charred grass and sticks

And an old fire-fragrance lingering on,
Erotic woodsmoke, witchery, intrigue,
Leaving us none the wiser, just better primed
To speed the plough again and feed the flame.

At the Wellhead

Your songs, when you sing them with your two eyes
    closed
As you always do, are like a local road
We've known every turn of in the past—
That midge-veiled, high-hedged side-road where you
    stood
Looking and listening until a car
Would come and go and leave you lonelier
Than you had been to begin with. So, sing on,
Dear shut-eyed one, dear far-voiced veteran,

Sing yourself to where the singing comes from,
Ardent and cut off like our blind neighbour
Who played the piano all day in her bedroom.
Her notes came out to us like hoisted water
Ravelling off a bucket at the wellhead
Where next thing we'd be listening, hushed and
    awkward.

·

That blind-from-birth, sweet-voiced, withdrawn
    musician
Was like a silver vein in heavy clay.
Night water glittering in the light of day.
But also just our neighbour, Rosie Keenan.
She touched our cheeks. She let us touch her braille

In books like books wallpaper patterns came in.
Her hands were active and her eyes were full
Of open darkness and a watery shine.

She knew us by our voices. She'd say she 'saw'
Whoever or whatever. Being with her
Was intimate and helpful, like a cure
You didn't notice happening. When I read
A poem with Keenan's well in it, she said,
'I can see the sky at the bottom of it now.'

At Banagher

Then all of a sudden there appears to me
The journeyman tailor who was my antecedent:
Up on a table, cross-legged, ripping out

A garment he must recut or resew,
His lips tight back, a thread between his teeth,
Keeping his counsel always, giving none,

His eyelids steady as wrinkled horn or iron.
Self-absenting, both migrant and ensconced;
Admitted into kitchens, into clothes

His touch has the power to turn to cloth again—
All of a sudden he appears to me,
Unopen, unmendacious, unillumined.

                              ·

So more power to him on the job there, ill at ease
Under my scrutiny in spite of years
Of being inscrutable as he threaded needles

Or matched the facings, linings, hems and seams.
He holds the needle just off centre, squinting,
And licks the thread and licks and sweeps it through,

Then takes his time to draw both ends out even,
Plucking them sharply twice. Then back to stitching.
Does he ever question what it all amounts to

Or ever will? Or care where he lays his head?
My Lord Buddha of Banagher, the way
Is opener for your being in it.

Tollund

That Sunday morning we had travelled far.
We stood a long time out in Tollund Moss:
The low ground, the swart water, the thick grass
Hallucinatory and familiar.

A path through Jutland fields. Light traffic sound.
Willow bushes; rushes; bog-fir grags
In a swept and gated farmyard; dormant quags.
And silage under wraps in its silent mound.

It could have been a still out of the bright
'Townland of Peace', that poem of dream farms
Outside all contention. The scarecrow's arms
Stood open opposite the satellite

Dish in the paddock, where a standing stone
Had been resituated and landscaped,
With tourist signs in *futhark* runic script
In Danish and in English. Things had moved on.

It could have been Mulhollandstown or Scribe.
The byroads had their names on them in black
And white; it was user-friendly outback
Where we stood footloose, at home beyond the tribe,

More scouts than strangers, ghosts who'd walked
        abroad

Unfazed by light, to make a new beginning
And make a go of it, alive and sinning,
Ourselves again, free-willed again, not bad.

September 1994

Postscript

And some time make the time to drive out west
Into County Clare, along the Flaggy Shore,
In September or October, when the wind
And the light are working off each other
So that the ocean on one side is wild
With foam and glitter, and inland among stones
The surface of a slate-grey lake is lit
By the earthed lightning of a flock of swans,
Their feathers roughed and ruffling, white on white,
Their fully grown headstrong-looking heads
Tucked or cresting or busy underwater.
Useless to think you'll park and capture it
More thoroughly. You are neither here nor there,
A hurry through which known and strange things pass
As big soft buffetings come at the car sideways
And catch the heart off guard and blow it open.